AFRIKAANS CHILDREN'S BOOK

YOUR CHILD'S FIRST 30 WORDS

ILLUSTRATED BY:
FEDERICO BONIFACINI

ROAN WHITE

TEACH YOUR CHILDREN ALL THE
NEW WORDS THEY NEED TO LEARN
EARLY WITH THIS BOOK.

INCLUDING 30 OF THE MOST USEFUL,
FUN, HAPPY WORDS, THIS COLORFUL,
GORGEOUSLY ILLUSTRATED BOOK WILL
BREATHE HAPPINESS AND PASSION FOR
LANGUAGE INTO YOUR CHILD'S LIFE.

FROM MOM TO APPLE TO DOG TO RAIN
TO PUDDLE, THIS BOOK BRINGS ALL
THESE WORDS INTO YOUR KIDS LIFE
THROUGH GORGEOUS ILLUSTRATIONS.

ALL VOCABULARY IS IN AFRIKAANS.

MA

PA

APPELTERT

SJOKOLADE

JOGURT

PANNEKOEK

DRUKKIE

VOËL

WATER

STERRE

HOND

KAT

BOEK

POP

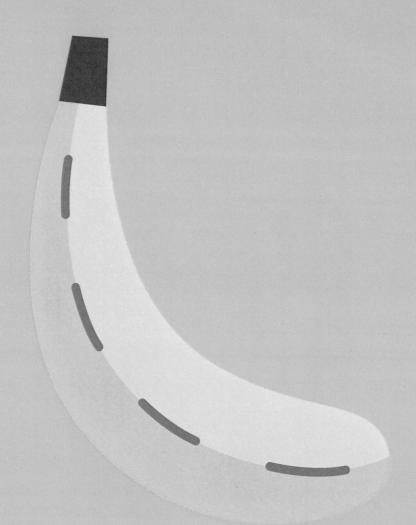

PIESANG

AARBEI

GLY

HOENDER

PLAS

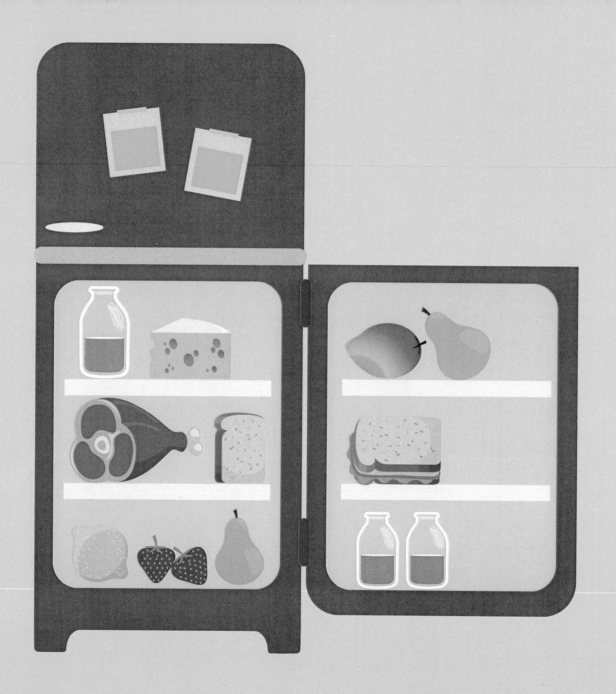

YSKAS

REKENAAR

REËN

REËNBOOG

SOEN

KAR

HUIS

VLIEGTUIG

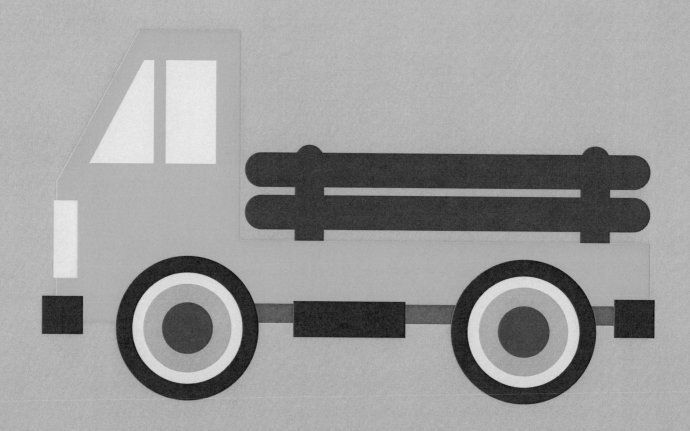

TROK

KRYT

SAND

11421751R00020

Made in the USA
San Bernardino, CA
04 December 2018